IF

Γ

Greater Than a Tourist Book Series
Reviews from Readers

I think the series is wonderful and beneficial for tourists to get information before visiting the city.

-Seckin Zumbul, Izmir Turkey

I am a world traveler who has read many trip guides but this one really made a difference for me. I would call it a heartfelt creation of a local guide expert instead of just a guide.

-Susy, Isla Holbox, Mexico

New to the area like me, this is a must have!

 -Joe, Bloomington, USA

This is a good series that gets down to it when looking for things to do at your destination without having to read a novel for just a few ideas.

-Rachel, Monterey, USA

Good information to have to plan my trip to this destination.

-Pennie Farrell, Mexico

Great ideas for a port day.

-Mary Martin USA

Aptly titled, you won't just be a tourist after reading this book. You'll be greater than a tourist!

-Alan Warner, Grand Rapids, USA

Even though I only have three days to spend in San Miguel in an upcoming visit, I will use the author's suggestions to guide some of my time there. An easy read - with chapters named to guide me in directions I want to go.

-Robert Catapano, USA

Great insights from a local perspective! Useful information and a very good value!

-Sarah, USA

This series provides an in-depth experience through the eyes of a local. Reading these series will help you to travel the city in with confidence and it'll make your journey a unique one.

-Andrew Teoh, Ipoh, Malaysia

GREATER THAN A TOURIST- MARYLAND USA

50 Travel Tips from a Local

Amber Montgomery

Cover designed by: Ivana Stamenkovic
Cover Image: https://pixabay.com/en/baltimore-harbor-boats-marina-1003183/

CZYK Publishing Since 2011.

Greater Than a Tourist
Visit our website at www.GreaterThanaTourist.com

Lock Haven, PA
ISBN: 9781723983955

> TOURIST

50 TRAVEL TIPS FROM A LOCAL

BOOK DESCRIPTION

Are you excited about planning your next trip?

Do you want to try something new?

Would you like some guidance from a local?

If you answered yes to any of these questions, then this Greater Than a Tourist book is for you.

Greater Than a Tourist- Maryland by Amber Montgomery offers the inside scoop on the state of Maryland. Most travel books tell you how to travel like a tourist. Although there is nothing wrong with that, as part of the Greater Than a Tourist series, this book will give you travel tips from someone who has lived at your next travel destination.

In these pages, you will discover advice that will help you throughout your stay. This book will not tell you exact addresses or store hours but instead will give you excitement and knowledge from a local that you may not find in other smaller print travel books.

Travel like a local. Slow down, stay in one place, and get to know the people and the culture. By the time you finish this book, you will be eager and prepared to travel to your next destination.

TABLE OF CONTENTS

DEDICATION

This book is dedicated to my mom and dad for giving me life and teaching me how to live it.

ABOUT THE AUTHOR

Amber Montgomery is a freelance writer who lives in Baltimore, Maryland. She was born and raised in Pasadena, Maryland and left the state in 2013 to attend college at the University of Pittsburgh, where she studied History and Arabic and began her writing career as an opinions columnist and editor at The Pitt News. After graduating, she moved to Amman, Jordan to teach English as a Second Language for a year where she cultivated her love of English and writing even further.

After five years away, she returned home to Maryland in 2018 because she believes it to be the best state in the U.S. and where she wants to live the rest of her life. In her free time, she loves to cook, read and travel. Contact her at montgomeryamber6@gmail.com or connect with her on Twitter @president_amber.

HOW TO USE THIS BOOK

The Greater Than a Tourist book series was written by someone who has lived in an area for over three months. The goal of this book is to help travelers either dream or experience different locations by providing opinions from a local. The author has made suggestions based on their own experiences. Please do your own research before traveling to the area in case the suggested places are unavailable.

FROM THE PUBLISHER

Traveling can be one of the most important parts of a person's life. The anticipation and memories that you have are some of the best. As a publisher of the Greater Than a Tourist book series, as well as the popular 50 Things to Know book series, we strive to help you learn about new places, spark your imagination, and inspire you. Wherever you are and whatever you do I wish you safe, fun, and inspiring travel.

Lisa Rusczyk Ed. D.
CZYK Publishing

OUR STORY

Traveling is a passion of the "Greater than a Tourist" series creator. Lisa studied abroad in college, and for their honeymoon Lisa and her husband toured Europe. During her travels to Malta, an older man tried to give her some advice based on his own experience living on the island since he was a young boy. She was not sure if she should talk to the stranger but was interested in his advice. When traveling to some places she was wary to talk to locals because she was afraid that they weren't being genuine. Through her travels, Lisa learned how much locals had to share with tourists. Lisa created the "Greater Than a Tourist" book series to help connect people with locals. A topic that locals are very passionate about sharing.

WELCOME TO
> TOURIST

INTRODUCTION

"The real voyage of discovery consists not in seeing new landscapes, but in having new eyes."

–Marcel Proust

While there are few comforts I find more close to my heart than sleeping in my own bed and waking up to my dogs, I still find travel to be one of the great passions of my life. Born and raised in Maryland, I moved away to attend college in Pittsburgh. There, while I missed my home, I learned so much more about the world and myself. I studied abroad two summers in college, trips that took me to Jordan, Palestine, Israel, Germany and England. After graduating college, I lived in Jordan for a year and backpacked through Italy afterwards as well. Whenever I travel, there's always a little piece of me missing home and wishing I could bring everyone and everything from home with me on my journeys to share with them.

But when I return home and unpack my bag and everything settles, I always feel more connected to home having returned to it with new experiences and fresh eyes. I've learned to cherish both things — the exploring of new places and the comfort of returning home. So when I got the chance to write a book about people who want to travel to my home, I was thrilled. I hope you enjoy this book and all my little tips and tricks for enjoying Maryland. Safe travels!

1. WHY VISIT

Although Maryland is one of the smallest states in the country, we're big on good people, good fun and having a good time. One of Maryland's most popular nicknames is America in Miniature. It's granted such a prestigious title because you really can experience almost all of what our great nation has to offer in one small state. Throughout the year, Marylanders experience each of the four seasons in turn and we've got mountains, green forests, caves, rolling farmlands, the Chesapeake Bay and the Atlantic Ocean all within our borders — and all only a few hours drive away. The state's geographic location just south of the Mason-Dixon line makes it a cultural blend of America's north and south where you can find seafood galore as well as southern style barbeque. The part the Old Line State plays in American history — home to the Battle of Antietam and the birthplace of the Star Spangled Banner at Fort McHenry — is unparalleled as well. Its bustling cities like Baltimore, Annapolis, and Bethesda combined with the plethora of small, charming towns means your trip to Maryland will be full of unique and diverse experiences and you'll never be without something to do or explore.

2. BEST TIMES TO VISIT

Maryland is a state that consistently enjoys each of the four seasons throughout the year. So if you plan to visit in the summer months, expect summer heat and summer crowds near the beaches and waterways. In fall and winter, things will slow down but you'll also need to be prepared for colder weather. Each season, of course, has advantages and disadvantages. If you're a beach person, visit in the summer but be sure to book ahead of time and be mentally prepared for crowds and physically prepared for the heat and humidity. And while we don't get huge snowstorms often, the winter months can still be quite frigid. While you're sure to have a good time anytime, if you have the choice, it's best to visit in the late spring or early fall. During this time the weather will be ideal without being unbearable and kids will either still be in or just be starting school so most families will be home during the week, lessening the crowds at more popular locations.

3. WHAT TO PACK

Of course what clothes to bring depends on the season but also what you plan on doing. Bear in mind that much of Maryland in the summertime is hot and humid, but near the ocean the humidity vanishes significantly and it can even get chilly at night in the spring and early summer. There's no shortage of sunshine in Maryland either, especially in the summer, so be sure to pack hats and plenty of sunblock. If you plan on hiking or exploring nature, it's a good idea to bring appropriate clothing and footwear and high socks, as ticks are common (but be sure to check yourself afterwards no matter what you wear!). If you're visiting in the winter months, a heavy coat isn't a must but will come in handy if the temperatures drop. Rain is fairly common year round in Maryland, especially during hurricane season, as edges of storms headed for the east coast tend to brush parts of Maryland, so it's good to keep a raincoat nearby as well.

In terms of formality, Marylanders are fairly casual in our dress. If you're planning on going to a upscale restaurant or a show, something a bit fancier might be appropriate. But other than, whatever you're

17

most comfortable in will be best as you explore the Old Line State. Just be careful about donning a Pittsburgh Steelers jersey on a game day, that one might get you into some trouble!

4. HIT THE CASH MACHINE

Even in the age of chip readers and Apple pay, it's never a bad idea to have some cash on hand. And while you'll be able to use credit or debit at most major tourist destinations and restaurants, if you plan on exploring some of Maryland's small towns and back roads, it's much less common to be able to swipe for your purchases. ATMs are, of course, widely found all throughout the state but consider stopping by one to grab some bills if you're planning to head to the Eastern Shore or a small town. You'll find stands along the way selling fresh fruits and veggies, nuts, and pies almost every few miles and you'll want to have some cash on hand if you feel like indulging in a locally grown snack.

5. WHERE TO GO

Depending on how long you plan to stay in Maryland will affect where you plan to go. If you're looking to just hit the highlights, you can't miss spending at least one day and night in Baltimore, Annapolis and somewhere on the Eastern Shore with a day trip to Ocean City included if possible.

If you have a little longer to stay, check out other small towns throughout the state, such as Berlin, St. Michaels or Chesapeake City for a relaxing stay in a guesthouse or Bed and Breakfast. With more time and depending on your interests, there are smaller cities, like Hagerstown or Frederick, to be explored as well as numerous parks and wildlife centers for walks and hikes.

6. WHERE TO STAY

I can't suggest AirBnb enough to any traveler, no matter where they are going! It's lovely to stay in a place that feels more like a home than a stuffy hotel room and it's a great way to meet and interact with locals! If you plan on staying a night in Baltimore, check out the site for people renting out rooms or entire apartments — particularly in one of the hipper, walking friendly parts of the city like Canton, Brewer's Hill, Fell's Point or Federal Hill. You'll save money, be in a more convenient area and probably pick up some great tips about what to check out from your hosts.

For Annapolis, I'd recommend splurging a bit to stay at one of the historic inns or taverns in downtown Annapolis — be sure to ask about the story behind the place when you check in — so you'll be walking distance from the harbor, cool bars, fabulous restaurants, and the Maryland State House. If you want to visit Ocean City in the summertime, there are plenty of hotels, motels, and apartments to choose from for varying costs, just be sure to book ahead of time! If you're looking to head to the beach on a budget, look at places to stay in Ocean Pines, Berlin or Salisbury where you can drive into the city for the day and stay at a more affordable place. And finally if you have time to explore some of Maryland's quaint towns on the Eastern Shore, I'd recommend looking up local inns or Bed and Breakfasts for a quaint and relaxing time.

7. HOW LONG TO STAY

As long as you like, of course! Marylanders love sharing their state pride with others, both people born and raised here and newcomers. Realistically you can see most of the highlights the state has to offer in a three to four days but you can catch many of the other hidden gems if you plan to stay a week. If you're looking for a longer-term stay, there are local Marylanders who rent out homes in small towns, the suburbs or in Ocean City for affordable rates while they head north for the summer or south for the winter.

8. PLANNING YOUR STAY

If you plan to go with a four-day trip, I'd suggest spending the first day and night in Baltimore. Next, head out early to hang out in Annapolis for the day before crossing the Bay Bridge to stay the night in a small B&B in an Eastern Shore town. Wake up and explore a bit before driving the rest of the way to Ocean City for a beach day and night. Head back west for your final day and spend it how you fancy —

21

take a hike, visit a historical place, or trek over to our nation's capital. For a longer stay, extend your time in each place — maybe catch a Orioles game or explore museums in Baltimore and visit Assateague Island while in Ocean City — and spend a day or two in western Maryland exploring some of the local nature parks and hikes.

9. HOW TO GET AROUND

If you're flying into Maryland, Baltimore-Washington International airport — a.k.a. BWI — is going to be your best choice. Unless you're planning to explore D.C. first, BWI will be much closer to most of your destinations in the Old Line State. From there, renting a car is the best way to be able to explore the whole state as you can easily drive from one side to the other in a matter of hours. For transportation within cities, parking can sometimes be difficult but Uber and Lyft are very prominent throughout populated areas. There is a light rail and bus system in Baltimore for travelers on a budget but be aware that it can be unreliable. If you're looking to get into D.C. or if you're flying into Reagan or Dulles

airports, the D.C. metro is good and reliable option
that will get you into western Maryland but doesn't
extend that far into the state so you'll need further
transportation to get around.

10. LOOK INTO E-Z PASS

If you already have an E-Z Pass from your own
state, you can use it the same way in Maryland. If you
don't have one but you plan to do a lot of traveling in
the Midwest and Eastern parts of the U.S., it might be
worth the investment as it saves you time and money
on many tolls. Some of the major highways in
Maryland have tolls and you can use your E-Z Pass to
breeze through them more quickly — but the number
one place E-Z Pass becomes the most valuable here is
at the Bay Bridge. If you're traveling on a weekend in
summer or even during rush hour times during the
week, traffic on the Bridge can be a real headache and
a huge time drain. Although there are now two
bridges when there used to be only one, it still takes
time for all the cars to pay the toll, merge down into
the few lanes and cross — plus there is often
inevitable accidents that slow it down even further.

Having an E-Z Pass ready to go at the Bridge can help save time and get you across the 4.3 miles of bridge much quicker (and you'll pay $2.50 instead of the full price of $4.00).

11. PLAN AHEAD

As with any trip, having a schedule is the key to success and maximizing time. Knowing when and where you will be driving and taking into account Maryland's traffic patterns can save you a lot of time as you go from Point A to B. If you're going to be around the D.C. area, avoid driving during rush hour times when working Marylanders will be flowing into and out of the city — nothing south of the Mason-Dixon line rivals D.C. traffic! The same applies for driving near Baltimore and Annapolis but to a lesser extent. If you're headed across the Bay Bridge to get to the Eastern Shore, be aware that the Bridge is the main roadway connecting the two Maryland shores and traffic tends to build up during weekend transit hours — Friday nights and Saturday mornings eastbound and Sunday nights westbound — and traditional rush hours. A tip: if driving across bridges makes you nervous, be sure to stay left when crossing the bridge eastbound as they tend to open one of the lanes on the opposite bridge to make traffic go faster.

12. LEARN SOME PHRASES

As with any state, Marylanders have a few key words that might stump you if you're not used to them. If you hear someone asking you "how bout dem Ohs?," they're referring to the Birds of Baltimore, the Orioles! If you head farther south, you might hear people calling you 'dear' or 'darling' but in Maryland, the most popular of these is the Baltimore originated 'hon.' If you hear someone asking you, "how you doing today, hon?" it might sound odd but they're just being friendly and expressing their endearment! On the other end of the spectrum, you might hear folks jokingly calling you a 'chicken necker,' especially on the Eastern Shore. This is a slang term used by locals for tourists in Maryland as it was easy to identify people from out of town because they'd be using chicken necks to catch crabs.

And geographically, Maryland is often lumped together with the surrounding states that make up the

Mid-Atlantic region of the U.S., and we Marylanders embrace this idea. The term 'DMV' or 'Delmarva' might sound like where you go to get your driver's license renewed (we call that the MVA in Maryland!), but it's just the way the locals refer to the region that is Delaware, Maryland and Virginia — by taking the first letters/sounds of each of the states, get it? Remember this one, you'll see it on store signs and bumper stickers, hear it on the radio, and you might even pass by Perdue Stadium in Salisbury, home to the minor league Delmarva Shorebirds.

13. SAYING HI

When I visit other states around the country, I sometimes find that being friendly with strangers around town is seen as a little odd. In some small pockets of Maryland, you might find people like that — such as on the D.C. metro as tired staffers, lawyers and professionals make their way from their Maryland homes to their D.C. work each morning. But for the most part, people in Maryland tend to take life slow and simply. They enjoy saying hi and smiling at people they see out on the street or in the supermarket. People won't normally walk up and start telling you their life story but folks will stop to say hi and perhaps comment on something nearby, so don't be alarmed! If you'd rather not talk, just smile and nod, no one will be offended. But if you're the talkative type too, feel free to strike up conversations and ask questions, most of the time people will be happy to chat with you for a bit. This is also a great way to get recommendations from locals as well, so if you're feeling it, don't be afraid to embrace it!

14. LEARN THE DIALECT TOO

While Marylanders do have a few funny words for ordinary things, just as important to know is the way we say certain words. You won't find many natives with a complete southern drawl but there is definitely an accent most Marylanders carry that sets them apart from other Americans. You'll hear people say 'warsh,' when they mean 'wash' and refer to our great state of Maryland as 'Merlin' or to Baltimore as "Bawlmoor." Days of the week are not really 'days' here but 'dees.' For example, where many people would say 'Sunday' and 'Monday,' you'll often hear it pronounced as 'Sundee' and 'Mondee' here, drawing out that last sound so it's just the letter 'd'.

My personal favorite? When Marylanders tend to take common questions and jumble the words together so that 'did you eat yet?' becomes 'ja'et yet?' or when asking someone what they did this weekend, they reply, 'went downee osheen' to imply they went down to the Ocean!

15. AND THE NICKNAMES!

And of course just as Texas is well known for being The Lone Star State and Chicago is The Windy City, Maryland also has nicknames for itself and many of its major places. The Old Line State — the nickname you see for Maryland on its state quarter along side the State House — is a name that originates from George Washington. It's said that General Washington referred to the Maryland soldiers who stood and fought at the state line during the Revolutionary War as "The Old Line." A local newspaper editor first used another popular nickname, The Free State, at the Baltimore Sun in editorials — and for some reason, the name stuck.

While in Baltimore, you'll see no shortage of delis and bakeries named after its famous nicknames of Charm City or Smalltimore. And Annapolis, a former capital of the U.S., is often affectionately called both Crabtown and Naptown.

16. BRUSHING UP ON HISTORY

Marylanders take great pride in everything their state has to offer and this includes its rich history as well. In high school, Maryland history was an elective almost every student took — in my case, taught by the head football coach of course. Knowing a bit about the background of Maryland will make your experience all the richer as you notice names and references to some of Maryland's greatest founders, residents and events throughout your journey. Its name was given to honor King Charles I wife, Queen Mary. Settled by Sir George Calvert in 1634, Maryland later became the seventh state to ratify the Constitution in 1788. Famous Maryland natives in history include Frederick Douglass, Francis Scott Key, Edward Allen Poe, Babe Ruth, and Harriet Tubman.

17. KNOW YOUR COUNTIES

Almost every state has counties to split up their land into more digestible regions and so Maryland does to. While natives take great pride in their state, they also live and die by their counties as well. For Marylanders, living in a different county can sometimes be akin to living in entirely different countries. After graduation, my sister's college boyfriend moved to a different county for his new job — and it's safe to say the relationship didn't last much longer!

Don't be surprised to see county pride bumper stickers or to stumble upon a huge county fair while in Maryland. And if you hear people referring to countries by nicknames, it's normal; it just may take you a minute to decipher what they mean. Some to know: HoCo = Howard County, MoCo = Montgomery County, PG = Prince George's and my hometown, AA = Anne Arundel.

18. GRAB SOME BUG SPRAY

If you've ever been to Washington D.C. in the summer months, you know just how humid and swampy it can get — think the Everglades minus the actual swamp. Maryland is similar during the hotter days of the year in many parts. While we appreciate our unique environment and the creatures that come along with it, it also means enduring mosquitos, moths, and other bugs every now and again. Be sure to pack some bug spray and maybe some citronella candles, or pick them up when you get here, to help keep the pests away. You won't be swarmed without it but you don't want an outside meal or adventure ruined by not having it either!

19. MARYLAND BLUE CRABS

Here it is, the big kahuna! Chesapeake Bay Blue Crabs are probably what Maryland is most famous for in the United States. And you can't visit Maryland without at least having a taste of our crabs. Of course I would recommend a traditional crab feast as the way to go. This would include all-you-can-eat crabs, corn, shrimp, potato salad, hush puppies, and butter. Forget any plans you had for the rest of the day and just sit back and relax as the locals teach you how to pick crabs and devour the meat. Eat them plain, dipped in butter and Old Bay, or soaked in vinegar. Don't forget to throw in a few pitchers of ice-cold beer as well. Mallets will be included, so whack away!

If cracking open and picking crabs for hours on end isn't exactly what you picture on your ideal vacation, don't fret. We'll forgive you! There are plenty of other ways to enjoy Maryland crabs without so much effort. For soup lovers, cream of crab or Maryland crab are two soups you'll find in any traditional Maryland restaurant — or even try my favorite way of doing it: a cup of half and half that mixes the two soups together. Enjoy a lump crab cake to get the taste of crabs without the effort of picking or order crab dip — a combination of crab meat and cheese baked and enjoyed on chips or bread. Or if you just want to add some crab to your traditional eats, you'll find crabby twists on every meal imaginable in most Maryland restaurants — including crab meat on a burger, in a quesadilla, on nachos, or in a jalapeno popper. Don't forget to pile on the Old Bay, a traditional Maryland seasoning for seafood made up of celery salt, black pepper, paprika, and red pepper flakes.

20. WHAT TO EAT

Now that we've covered the absolute necessity of how to experience crabs in Maryland, we can also move on to other Maryland must-try foods. While crabs are many Maryland natives' number one choice, there is also a plethora of other fresh seafood to be found on a daily basis. You'll find no shortage of seafood restaurants hosting fresh oysters, scallops, rockfish and shrimp.

If you're more of a meat lover, Maryland is famous for pit beef as well. You can't go wrong with this choice, whether it's at a food truck, roadside stall or a diner. Pit Beef is Maryland's own twist on American barbeque: basically a tender roast beef sandwich that's been cooked with charcoal to retain a heavenly smoky flavor.

While hanging on the beach or strolling the boardwalk in Ocean City, don't miss out on two traditional favorites — Thrasher's fries, served with salt and vinegar, and Fisher's caramel popcorn.

Finally for dessert, our official state dessert is the Smith Island Cake — a delicacy layered with thin yellow cake and fudgy chocolate icing.

21. MARYLAND PIZZA

While we're on the topic of food, let's talk pizza. While New York and Chicago are known for their famous pizzas, Maryland also has a small slice in the game of pizza. Real Marylanders know that the best pizza comes in square form. First opened near the University of Maryland, the now famous Ledo's Pizza has stretched across the Mid-Atlantic and has been serving up its delicious and signature square pizzas since 1955. Try a traditional pepperoni where each box-shaped slice comes is topped with one thick slice of pepperoni!

22. WHAT TO DRINK

Surrounded by water in many places, one of any Marylander's favorite pastimes is sitting near the water and indulging in a few adult beverages. You'd be hard pressed to find any respectable bar in Maryland that doesn't serve the Free State's signature cocktail — the orange crush. Always made with freshly squeezed orange juice, vodka and triple sec the traditional drink is also often now served in grapefruit and other flavors too. Also found frequently throughout the state but an absolute staple in any Baltimore bar is the Maryland beer, National Bohemian — or Natty Boh for short. First brewed in 1885, you can enjoy a Natty Boh in a can but I prefer it on draft with the rim of the glass coated in Old Bay! Another tip: While in Baltimore, keep an eye out for the Natty Boh face atop a tower in Brewer's hill! If you look long enough, he'll surely wink at you!

23. GRABBING SNACKS

No trip to Maryland is complete without picking up a few snacks to munch on throughout your days. Pick up some Berger cookies while in Baltimore to keep you in a sugar high as you drive to your next destination. The cookie was first brought to Baltimore from Germany and features a vanilla cookie topped with a generous amount of thick, chocolate fudge. If you prefer salty to sweet, crab a bag of crab flavored snacks — most grocery stores will have at least once brand of crab chips, crisps, and even cheese balls.

As you're crusin' down Route 50 to Ocean City, be sure to stop at the local produce stalls for fresh watermelon and corn. And if you're visiting in the summer, be sure to seek out a local snowball stand to taste Maryland's twist on the American sno cone. Rather than flavored shaved ice served in a small paper cup you may be thinking of, a Maryland snowball is served in a Styrofoam cup and loaded with syrup and marshmallow fluff.

24. FAMILY FUN

There's something for people of all ages in Maryland but there's no doubting that American families love heading to the Old Line State for fun trips where they can spend quality time with their loved ones. The National Aquarium in Baltimore's Inner Harbor is a crowd pleaser for moms, dads, kids, and grandparents! Wonder through the maze of tanks and water to see jellyfish, sharks, and the 500-pound Green Sea Turtle Calypso. Take a trip to Fort

McHenry ⌐— the fort that inspired the writing of our national anthem in 1812 — to teach the kids a bit more about American history. Or challenge each other to a game of Miniature Golf after spending the day surfing the waves and tanning in Ocean City. At night, take in a show or a movie at the New Embassy Theatre in Cumberland or at Bengies Drive-In Theatre in Middle River.

25. EXPLORING BALTIMORE

You can't visit Maryland without at least a stop off in the state's biggest city. During the day, check out the Inner Harbor, Babe Ruth's Birthplace and Museum, or Port Discovery — an interactive museum for kids. At night, find a local restaurant or bar in Canton or Fells Point for dinner and have a stroll around the water. If you have the time, take in a game at Oriole Park at Camden Yards to watch the Baltimore Orioles in action and see the 'ballpark that forever changed baseball.' If you have time in the mid-morning, Baltimore has embraced the country's new obsession with brunch in one of the best ways possible. Enjoy mimosas at one of the dozen restaurants overlooking the water in Fell's Point for a relaxing and refreshing morning.

26. WELCOME TO ANNAPOLIS

Visit the U.S. Naval Academy and its museum or take a tour of the State House and walk in the footsteps of George Washington. Enjoy a wonderful dinner and drinks at a restaurant downtown, preferable right on the water and watch the boats go in and out of the harbor. Do a pub-crawl or enjoy a ghost tour of historic Annapolis post-dinner to get a better feel for the city and explore.

27. THE BEST OF OCEAN CITY

Ocean City — or OC, for short — is a classic resort town located where the Chesapeake Bay meets the Atlantic Ocean. There are about 7,000 locals in the city but during peak summer weekends, the population can rise to upwards of 350,000. While it can get crowded during those times, the 9 mile beach that extends just south of the Delaware line is always open to visitors. During the day, enjoy the beach and grab lunch at a small deli or sandwich place for a picnic. At night, visit one of the city's numerous restaurants or bars or explore the 2.5 miles of boardwalk to people watch, shop or visit the rides and arcades in the inlet area.

28. TAKING A DIP

Seeing as Maryland is nearly cut in half by the Chesapeake Bay there is no shortage of ways to access the water here. If you don't want to make the trek over to Ocean City, there's still plenty of ways to enjoy the Bay closer to central part of the state. Sandy Point State Park hosts a recreational beach open to the public right alongside the Chesapeake Bay Bridge. You can bring or rent canoes or kayaks and take them for a ride at any neighborhood boating ramp or inlet. Or if you prefer lakes to bays and oceans, spend a night or two in the cabins lining Deep Creek Lake in Garrett County.

29. NIGHT LIFE

There's no shortage of nightlife in Maryland.
Anywhere you go you'll find restaurant and bars
filling up after dark with locals out to have fun and
socialize. In Baltimore, young professionals tend to
gather in Fell's Point or Fed Hill where the bars are
all walking distance from one another — and they can
defer driving in favor of a water taxi from
neighborhood to neighborhood instead! Visit the
famous Pickles Pub before or during an Orioles game
to see Baltimore natives in their natural habitat and
celebrate the O's with the bar's trademark pickle shot.
Across the Inner Harbor lies Power Plant Live a good
bar and restaurant in the city for live music. For a
wild night out, check out Cancun Cantina in either
Hagerstown or Hanover for a club with multiple bars,
a restaurant, pool tables, and dance floors. Or if
gambling is more your vibe, Maryland Live! Casino
in Arundel Mills is open 24/7 and features slots, table
games, gourmet restaurants, and live music.

30. KNOW YOUR BIRDS

There is a very slim chance you'll visit Maryland and not have someone bring up the topics of either the Ravens or the Orioles. If you're planning on wearing paraphernalia from an opposing team, you're welcome to but be prepared for people to comment on it! Be aware of heading into bars and restaurants during football hours as you're likely to find either good or poor spirits depending on how the team is fairing. Either way, though, you're bound to find beer and food specials during game times and enthusiastic Marylanders willing to share their love for their state with you.

31. MARYLAND SPORTS

While professional baseball and football are the main sports most Marylanders are obsessed with, there are also a number of other sports you'll find passion for as well. With the closest NHL team being the Washington Capitals, there's a small but very tight knit and dedicated Caps fan base throughout the state. And while locals take delight in high school

41

basketball and football to a certain extent, lacrosse is the sport that reigns most supreme among high schools sports in Maryland. And of course we can't forget about the state sport of Maryland: jousting! Admittedly, you're less likely to see that one in person but it's still a good fun fact to know!

32. SPENDING TIME IN NATURE

While most of Maryland is well known for waterways and beaches, there are also plenty of opportunities to abound in Maryland's natural resources that aren't water related. You can see native wildlife in the nature trails of Accokeek Farms at Piscataway Park or dig up fossils on the beaches of Calvert Cliffs State Park. If you like to hike, there are relaxing and smooth trails at Swallow Falls State Park or the Fort Foote Civil War Ruins Trail or challenge yourself to the 3-4 day hike of the 40-miles of Appalachian Trail that run through Maryland.

33. COOLING OFF INSIDE

If you're more of a house cat or are visiting during the winter or rain, there's plenty to do and see indoors throughout the state as well. The Maryland Science Center in Baltimore is fun for kids and adults alike with its exhibits, IMAX theatre, planetarium, and observatory. The Maryland Scenic Railroad is open rain or shine to take guests on a 3-hour train ride through Maryland's diverse landscape. The Annapolis Maritime Museum, the Baltimore Museum of Art, or the Star-Spangled Banner Flag House are all also fun ways to spend a day inside.

34. WAVE TO THE FLAG

Every state has its own little quirks, they're what make it unique and your friends and family are going to want to know what you saw in Maryland that makes it different from your home state. One thing you may notice is an awful lot of flags featuring yellow, black, red and white. This is, of course, the Maryland state flag and expect to see it everywhere! And I mean everywhere. Not just flying on flag poles

43

outside houses, hotels, or restaurants but you'll see people with bathing suits, hats, water bottles, car stickers and even tattoos resembling the iconic patterns of the flag. My mom's biggest pet peeve is seeing the Maryland flag upside down so keep an eye out and impress others with your Maryland knowledge if you see it flying the wrong way — the black and yellow should be in the upper left corner, i.e. where the stars are on the American flag!

35. SINGING THE NATIONAL ANTHEM

There's another very popular quirk you'll find in Maryland if you stay around long enough. It's one I feel inclined to mention because it can be startling if you're not aware of it. Most applicable at sporting events, bars or anywhere where singing may occur, it's how Marylanders add their own little state flair to our National Anthem. We all know that the Star-Spangled Banner begins with the iconic like of "O, say can you see." And as you'll probably recall, there's another 'O' in the second to the last line as well. On that line, locals shout the 'O' as loud as they can — as a reference and a nod to the local Baltimore team, the Orioles, more affectionately known as the O's.

As long as I can remember there's been a bit of controversy surrounding this particular Maryland tradition, as some say it's disrespectful to the National Anthem and our nation. But for us natives, it's just something we've all been doing to show our love for our state and express our uniqueness within this great country. Hopefully you'll be able to hear and experience this while you're in Maryland so you can decide for yourself how you feel about it!

36. A SCHOLARLY DETOUR

One very fond memory I have of traveling when I was younger is of my mom and I taking road trips to visit colleges up and down the east coast. If you've got a young student with you looking forward to their higher education or you just enjoy seeing places where the future of our country is cultivated, Maryland boasts more than enough colleges to stop in and see during your travels.

The University of Maryland is located in College Park, Maryland, about 8 miles northwest of Washington D.C. If you're coming from D.C. a mid-day stop for a few hours is all the time you need to see the school. Sign up to take a tour or wonder around on your own and see McKeldin Mall — modeled after the National Mall in D.C. — rub the foot of the great terrapin Testudo for good luck, and grab a scoop or two at the Dairy.

In Baltimore, a short detour can quickly bring you to the doors of Johns Hopkins University or one of the oldest art colleges in the country, the Maryland Institute College of Art. Another great and popular state university in Maryland is Towson, located in Baltimore County. Or if you have a beach lover with you, my sister's alma mater Salisbury University is located in a small town in Wicomico County, only 30 miles from the beach at Ocean City.

If you're near or planning to visit Washington D.C., don't forget about American, George Washington or Georgetown University either!

37. SMALL TOWN CHARM

The total area of Maryland is only about 12,000 square miles and with a population over 6 million, you might think much of the state is made up of city and suburb squished together to accommodate families, young people and D.C. workers who enjoy spending their free time in the Free State. While there are plenty of lovely suburbs throughout the state where families live idyllic lives, what makes Maryland a true encompassment of all of America is its small towns. While Baltimore and Annapolis are definitely sites you shouldn't miss, don't sleep on the sleepy towns of Maryland either.

Between D.C. and Baltimore lies a small town named Ellicott City, founded in 1772 and rumored to be haunted ever since. This town is full of historic charm, old stone mill buildings, and vintage stores before spending some time in one of the museums or restaurants.

Between Baltimore and Wilmington, where the Susquehanna River meets the Chesapeake Bay, is the peninsula town of Havre de Grace. Walk the boardwalk that runs from Tydings Park to the Concord Point Lighthouse and feel like you're in a small New England resort town. Hit the links for 18 holes at the beautiful Bulle Rock Golf Course or visit the Decoy Museum to see thousands of Chesapeake style waterfowl decoys.

On your way to Ocean City, make time to stop in Berlin for a quick visit or stay a night. Nothing like the bustling German metropolis, only about 4,500 people call Berlin, MD home. If you're in town in July, be sure to stop in to catch the town's annual Bathtub Race. At other times of the year, visit the Burley Oak Taproom for a pint of beer brewed organically and from indigenous Eastern Shore ingredients.

38. POP IN ON THE PONIES

If you peer south from the inlet in Ocean City, you might be able to spot a barrier island a few miles away. This 37-mile long strip of land, with the northern two-thirds belonging to Maryland, is Assateague Island — a popular destination known for beautiful beaches and herds of free roaming horses abound on the island. Legend says these horses descended from domestic horses that survived a shipwreck in the area in the 17th century. On the Maryland side of the island, you can watch the ponies roam, take a wildlife tour, or explore the water on either the ocean or bay sides.

39. A MIRACLE ON 34TH STREET

Who hasn't seen or at least heard of this famous Christmas movie from 1947? In the same year the movie was released, some Baltimore residents of their own 34th street decided to embrace the holiday spirit of the movie. Now, every year starting in late November, the houses on the 700 block of 34th Street in Baltimore's Hampden neighborhood put up an unparalleled display of holiday lights. The two and three story row houses with bay windows are decorated with lights, Disney characters, Hanukkah menorahs, Christmas trees, trains, Santas and Frostys, and several holiday themed homages to Baltimore. Local residents sell hot chocolate and other winter refreshments but the displays themselves are free and open to all. If you're in town during the holiday season, it's a one of a kind stop you can't miss!

40. TAKE A DAY TRIP TO THE NATION'S CAPITAL

While there's plenty to do to keep you busy for days on end in Maryland, if you have a day to spare, getting to Washington D.C. for a few hours is an easy and exciting addition to your vacation. Instead of battling traffic and paying an exuberant parking fee, park at a metro stop — New Carrollton, Greenbelt, or Largo Town Center are all in western Maryland — and have a pleasant ride into the city.

Explore the National Mall or take a tour of the Capitol Building and the Library of Congress, visit the Smithsonian museums and see the memorials along the National Mall, grab lunch and scope out the vendors selling crafts and goods at Eastern Market on Pennsylvania Avenue. If you're visiting near the holidays, make time for a stop across the Potomac at Arlington National Cemetery to pay your respects at the Tomb of the Unknown Soldier and see the holiday wreaths laid on the graves of our nation's heroes.

41. CHARTERING A BOAT

As you drive around the state, you might notice cars along the highway with small boats hitched along the back or see them parked in driveways in any given suburb. Surrounded by water on so many sides, the people of Maryland love to take to the water on a sunny day. If you don't have a boat or don't want to lug it along with you on your trip, there are plenty of companies who rent boats to locals and tourists to take out for a few hours or a whole day. Rent a pontoon boat and head out for a day drink and a little party or find something more akin to fishing and swimming. Do a little research before your trip to find the most convenient prices and locations and ask around when you arrive for any locals who may have tips.

42. DINING LOCALLY

While we all love the comfort of our favorite hometown or chain restaurants, nothing bad can come from checking out something new. While in Maryland, be sure to dine out at some state-specific places with food, atmospheres and experiences you can only get here. If you like unique bars, be sure to check out Nacho Mama's in either Baltimore or Towson and Seacrets in Ocean City. Polar opposites, Nacho Mama's dishes out delicious tacos, quesadillas and hubcap margaritas (yes, that's an actual hubcap full of margarita) where Seacrets features both waterfront and water-in tables on the bay side of Coastal Highway (yes, you can actually sit in the Chesapeake Bay while drinking and snacking).

Stop by Chaps Pit Beef in either Baltimore or Aberdeen for traditional Maryland pit beef and the Papermoon Diner in the Baltimore for a one-of-a-kind diner experience. For crabs and seafood, The Point Crab House and Grill in Annapolis and Thames Street Oyster House in Baltimore can't be beat both for their food and atmosphere.

43. SOUVENIRS TO TAKE HOME

If you want to recreate the taste of Maryland after returning home, you can easily find cans of Old Bay in any Maryland grocery store or shop — feel free to stock up as the seasoning won't go bad anytime soon. For knick-knacks or gifts, small Maryland state flags are easy to find in local shops as are painted crab shells that you can order with custom sayings on them. Grab a tee shirt from the University of Maryland or from your favorite restaurant stop in Ocean City for a memory you can wear. Or my personal favorite way to display my Maryland flag is with a bumper sticker in the shape of a crab designed with the Maryland flag inside — it's a combination of all the best things the Old Line State has to offer.

44. MARYLAND ON A BUDGET

In one way or another, traveling is always going to cost a bit more money then just staying at home. Whether it's paying for food, transportation or places to stay, traveling is a costly passion. But don't be fooled into thinking vacations and travel to Maryland is only for middle class families. There is indeed plenty to do in Maryland that is free or very cheap if you're looking to explore on a budget.

A few places we've already discussed — like Assateague Island and Swallow Falls State Park —

are free to visit. The beach is always free to enjoy and pack lunch and drinks so you're not tempted to buy when you get there. Other adventures to be had for a low price include visiting the largest ship graveyard on the East Coast at Mallow Bay, take a tour of the Days End Farm Horse Rescue in Wheaton, or take in a flick at the free drive-in movie theatre that pops up on North Beach in the fall. Both the Walters Art Museum and the Baltimore Museum of Art offer free admission in the city. If you plan on visiting Berlin, the Globe Theatre in town hosts live performances and art shows for reasonable prices and the Salisbury Zoo is a free admission only a 30-minute drive away. And fun and exploration is always great to do in groups, so get a pile of friends together to split the cost of lodging and transportation to make it a more affordable trip.

45. OBEY THE LAW

Every state has a few wacky laws and Maryland is no exception. If you plan to head to the movies in Baltimore, please do not take your pet lion with you. In Caroline County on the Eastern Shore, pretending to be able to predict the future can land you in jail for six months or with $100 fine. It's also illegal to eat while swimming in the ocean but, from my experience, I think you can probably get away with that one. Hopefully you weren't tempted to do any of these things in the first place but now you know the facts that can at most keep you out of trouble and at least make for fun road trip trivia.

46. PICTURES TO TAKE

When you get back home, family and friends are going to want to revisit your vacation with you and see the wonderful things you did and saw. What other way is there to do this if not through a collection of photos? So be sure to take pictures of everything that strikes you — scenic walks, sunsets over the water, cobblestoned streets — but here are a few ideas for truly memorable photo opportunities you can only find in Maryland.

First things first: the Maryland flag. What could make a picture a better reminder of your trip then including a state flag in it? Wave one in the wind as you hang out on the beach or find local flag poles that will surely be sporting one. If you're here in summer, Marylander's take pride in growing fields of sunflowers for locals and tourists alike to enjoy. You can visit them at Broom's Bloom Dairy in Bel Air, Rocky Point Creamery in Tuscarora, or The Sunflower Garden in Westminster. Both the harbors in Baltimore and Annapolis make for Instagram-able photo ops or take a family photo as you ride down the Ocean City boardwalk on rented double-benched bicycles.

47. PLACES TO WALK

If walking is a part of your daily routine, you might start to miss the motion while you're on vacation. But given Maryland's diverse terrain, there's always somewhere to walk for both fitness and to take in some of the state's nature. Dedicated walking trails, like BWI Trail, the Anacostia River Trail or the Baltimore Annapolis Trail, are popular spots for locals who like to walk. Walk the whole thing if you've got the time or just portions throughout your trip.

The Baltimore Harbor, downtown Annapolis, or Old Ellicott City are all great places to stroll while window shopping. If you'd prefer a cultivated walk in nature, visit the 22-acre Iris Garden in Monkton or to see rushing waterfalls, head to the border between Maryland and Virginia to see the Great Falls of the Potomac River.

48. PLACES TO SHOP

If you're looking to do some back to school or summer shopping while in Maryland, visit one of the clusters of outlet stores in Hagerstown, Hanover, or Queenstown. For a more scenic, quaint shopping trip, visit the main streets in Berlin, Cambridge, Mount Airy, or Havre de Grace. If the shops are calling to you and not the kids, Schoolhouse Earth in Friendsville features a free petting zoo to entertain the youngins while you search for anything from jewelry to food samples to Christmas decorations within the stores walls. For a touch of history as well, visit Lexington Market in Baltimore that's been standing strong since 1782, making it one of the oldest continuous markets in the world!

49. STAYING SAFE

While anywhere and doing anything, the thing you want most for yourself and your loved ones is always staying safe. While Baltimore city might have a reputation for being a crime-riddled and dangerous city, don't let the city's problems deter you from what would be a wonderful visit. Just like in any city in the world, staying safe is about being smart and alert — and as long as you do those two things, the odds of something harming you in Maryland are very low. In the city, staying where other people and tourists are is the key.

While crime is an issue in the city, much of it tends to happen in isolated areas, not during a busy day at the Inner Harbor. Perhaps what you'll see most frequently is locals asking for money on street corners — something not unique to Baltimore — and most people won't bother you after you give them some change or just ignore them. Other than that, do all those things you momma taught you as a kid — lock your car, don't flash your money or valuables around, stay in groups, and don't let fear ruin a good time and a new city for you.

Being safe in a state with so much water is also important. On popular beaches there are always lifeguards on duty during the day so heed their advice and swim only in places where they can keep a good eye on you. Shark and other aquatic animal attacks are very rare in Maryland but there are sightings sometimes, especially in the waters of the Atlantic Ocean. Never swim alone and preferable always swim somewhere where there is a trained professional who can help and advise you.

More commonly, the bigger threats to safety are the nature of the water itself. When swimming in the Bay, the water is very rarely clear enough to see to the bottom — meaning it can be hard to know how deep water is when not in it. Be mindful and careful of jumping into waters or playing around, as the water could be much shallower than anticipated. Likewise, the waters of the Atlantic Ocean can get very rough depending on the weather and time of year. In Ocean City, the main threat most people face is getting stuck in rip tides — or strong, offshore currents that can drag you down the beach in mere seconds. If you get caught in a rip tide, wave to the lifeguard to alert them and don't try to swim directly out of it. Instead, swim parallel to the beach and let the tide carry you, eventually you'll work your way out of it and be able to swim into shore safely, albeit a ways away from where you entered.

50. READ THE PAPER

There's no way to get to know a place like reading the local paper. What political crises or crime are Marylanders really worried about? How are they gearing up for the next month and what's going on? How are the local high school football teams doing? You'll get to see what people in Maryland really care about and how that news is reported to them everyday. The Maryland Gazette and the Baltimore Sun will give you the broad strokes of what's going on in the state but smaller, more regional papers will also show off their individual small town charms and let you see what it would be like to really live in Maryland.

TOP REASONS TO BOOK THIS TRIP

Experience everything: Family can't decide if they want to go to a beach hour or a mountain cabin? You can do it all in Maryland.

History: Visit and learn more about some of American history's most important moments.

The American Mix: Experience everything America has to offer in one small state, including the perfect mix between the cultures of the north and south.

a

BONUS BOOK

50 THINGS TO KNOW ABOUT PACKING LIGHT FOR TRAVEL

PACK THE RIGHT WAY EVERY TIME

AUTHOR: MANIDIPA BHATTACHARYYA

Edited by Melanie Howthorne

ABOUT THE AUTHOR

Manidipa Bhattacharyya is a creative writer and editor, with an
education in English literature and Linguistics. After working in the IT
industry for seven long years she decided to call it quits and follow her
heart instead. Manidipa has been ghost writing, editing, proof reading
and doing secondary research services for many story tellers and article
writers for about three years. She stays in Kolkata, India with her
husband and a busy two year old. In her own time Manidipa enjoys
travelling, photography and writing flash fiction.

Manidipa believes in travelling light and never carries anything that she
couldn't haul herself on a trip. However, travelling with her child
changed the scenario. She seemed to carry the entire world with her for
the baby on the first two trips. But good sense prevailed and she is
again working her way to becoming a light traveler, this time with a
kid.

INTRODUCTION

He who would travel happily
must travel light.

-Antoine de Saint-Exupéry

Travel takes you to different places from seas and mountains to deserts and much more. In your travels you get to interact with different people and their cultures. You will, however, enjoy the sights and interact positively with these new people even more, if you are travelling light.

When you travel light your mind can be free from worry about your belongings. You do not have to spend precious vacation time waiting for your luggage to arrive after a long flight. There is be no chance of your bags going missing and the best part is that you need not pay a fee for checked baggage.

People who have mastered this art of packing light will root for you to take only one carry-on, wherever you go. However, many people can find it really hard to pack light. More so if you are travelling with children. Differentiating between "must have" and "just in case" items is the starting point. There will be ample shopping avenues at your destination which are just waiting to be explored.

This book will show you 'packing' in a new 'light' –
pun intended – and help you to embrace light
packing practices for all of your future travels.

Off to packing!

DEDICATION

I dedicate this book to all the travel buffs that I know,
who have given me great insights into the contents of
their backpacks.

THE RIGHT TRAVEL GEAR

1. CHOOSE YOUR TRAVEL GEAR CAREFULLY

While selecting your travel gear, pick items that are
light weight, durable and most importantly, easy to
carry. There are cases with wheels so you can drag
them along – these are usually on the heavy side
because of the trolley. Alternatively a backpack that
you can carry comfortably on your back, or even a
duffel bag that you can carry easily by hand or sling
across your body are also great options. Whatever
you choose, one thing to keep in mind is that the
luggage itself should not weigh a ton, this will give
you the flexibility to bring along one extra pair of
shoes if you so desire.

2. CARRY THE MINIMUM NUMBER OF BAGS

Selecting light weight luggage is not everything. You need to restrict the number of bags you carry as well. One carry-on size bag is ideal for light travel. Most carriers allow one cabin baggage plus one purse, handbag or camera bag as long as it slides under the seat in front. So technically, you can carry two items of luggage without checking them in.

3. PACK ONE EXTRA BAG

Always pack one extra empty bag along with your essential items. This could be a very light weight duffel bag or even a sturdy tote bag which takes up minimal space. In the event that you end up buying a lot of souvenirs, you already have a handy bag to stuff all that into and do not have to spend time hunting for an appropriate bag.

I'm very strict with my packing and have everything in its right place. I never change a rule. I hardly use anything in the hotel room. I wheel my own wardrobe in and that's it.

Charlie Watts

CLOTHES & ACCESSORIES

4. PLAN AHEAD

Figure out in advance what you plan to do on your trip. That will help you to pick that one dress you need for the occasion. If you are going to attend a wedding then you have to carry formal wear. If not, you can ditch the gown for something lighter that will be comfortable during long walks or on the beach.

5. WEAR THAT JACKET

Remember that wearing items will not add extra luggage for your air travel. So wear that bulky jacket that you plan to carry for your trip. This saves space and can also help keep you warm during the chilly flight.

6. MIX AND MATCH

Carry clothes that can be interchangeably used to reinvent your look. Find one top that goes well with a couple of pairs of pants or skirts. Use tops, shirts and jackets wisely along with other accessories like a scarf or a stole to create a new look.

7. CHOOSE YOUR FABRIC WISELY

Stuffing clothes in cramped bags definitely takes its toll which results in wrinkles. It is best to carry wrinkle free, synthetic clothes or merino tops. This will eliminate the need for that small iron you usually bring along.

8. DITCH CLOTHES PACK UNDERWEAR

Pack more underwear and socks. These are the things that will give you a fresh feel even if you do not get a chance to wear fresh clothes. Moreover these are easy to wash and can be dried inside the hotel room itself.

9. CHOOSE DARK OVER LIGHT

While picking your clothes choose dark coloured ones. They are easy to colour coordinate and can last longer before needing a wash. Accidental food spills and dirt from the road are less visible on darker clothes.

10. WEAR YOUR JEANS

Take only one pair of Jeans with you, which you should wear on the flight. Remember to pick a pair that can be worn for sightseeing trips and is equally eloquent for dinner. You can add variety by adding light weight cargoes and chinos.

11. CARRY SMART ACCESSORIES

The right accessory can give you a fresh look even with the same old dress. An intelligent neck-piece, a couple of bright scarves, stoles or a sarong can be used in a number of ways to add variety to your clothing. These light weight beauties can double up as a nursing cover, a light blanket, beach wear, a modesty cover for visiting places of worship, and also makes for an enthralling game of peek-a-boo.

12. LEARN TO FOLD YOUR GARMENTS

Seasoned travellers all swear by rolling their clothes for compact and wrinkle free packing. Bundle packing, where you roll the clothes around a central object as if tying it up, is also a popular method of compact and wrinkle free packing. Stacking folded clothes one on top of another is a big no-no as it makes creases extreme and they are difficult to get rid of without ironing.

13. WASH YOUR DIRTY LAUNDRY

One of the ways to avoid carrying loads of clothes is to wash the clothes you carry. At some places you might get to use the laundry services or a Laundromat but if you are in a pinch, best solution is to wash them yourself. If that is the plan then carrying quick drying clothes is highly recommended, which most often also happen to be the wrinkle free variety.

14. LEAVE THOSE TOWELS BEHIND

Regular towels take up a lot of space, are heavy and take ages to dry out. If you are staying at hotels they will provide you with towels anyway. If you are travelling to a remote place, where the availability of towels look doubtful, carry a light weight travel towel of viscose material to do the job.

15. USE A COMPRESSION BAG

Compression bags are getting lots of recommendation now days from regular travellers. These are useful for saving space in your luggage when you have to pack bulky dresses. While packing for the return trip, get help from the hotel staff to arrange a vacuum cleaner.

FOOTWEAR

16. PUT ON YOUR HIKING BOOTS

If you have plans to go hiking or trekking during your trip, you will need those bulky hiking boots. The best way to carry them is to wear them on flight to save space and luggage weight. You can remove the boots once inside and be comfortable in your socks.

17. PICKING THE RIGHT SHOES

Shoes are often the bulkiest items, along with being the dainty if you are a female. They need care and take up a lot of space in your luggage. It is advisable therefore to pick shoes very carefully. If you plan to do a lot of walking and site seeing, then wearing a pair of comfortable walking shoes are a must. For more formal occasions you can carry durable, light weight flats which will not take up much space.

18. STUFF SHOES

If you happen to pack a pair of shoes, ensure you utilize their hollow insides. Tuck small items like rolled up socks or belts to save space. They will also be easy to find.

TOILETRIES

19. STASHING TOILETRIES

Carry only absolute necessities. Airline rules dictate that for one carry-on bag, liquids and gels must be in 3.4 ounce (100ml) bottles or less, and must be packed in a one quart zip-lock bag. If you are planning to stay in a hotel, the basic things will be provided for you. It's best is to buy the rest from the local market at your destination.

20. TAKE ALONG TAMPONS

Tampons are a hard to find item in a lot of countries. Figure out how many you need and pack accordingly. For longer stays you can buy them online and have them delivered to where you are staying.

21. GET PAMPERED BEFORE YOU TRAVEL

Some avid travellers suggest getting a pedicure and manicure just the day before travelling. This not only gives you a well kept look, you also save the trouble of packing nail polish. Remember, every little bit of weight reduced adds up.

ELECTRONICS

22. LUGGING ALONG ELECTRONICS

Electronics have a large role to play in our lives today. Most of us cannot imagine our lives away from our phones, laptops or tablets. However while travelling, one must consider the amount of weight these electronics add to our luggage. Thankfully smart phones come along with all the essentials tools like a camera, email access, picture editing tools and more. They are smart to the point of eliminating the need to carry multiple gadgets. Choose a smart phone that suits all your requirements and travel with the world in your palms or pocket.

23. REDUCE THE NUMBER OF CHARGERS

If you do travel with multiple electronic devices, you will have to bear the additional burden of carrying all their chargers too. Check if a single charger can be used for multiple devices. You might also consider investing in a pocket charger. These small devices support multiple devices while keeping you charged on the go.

24. TRAVEL FRIENDLY APPS

Along with smart phones come numerous apps, which are immensely helpful in our travels. You name it and you have an app for it at hand – take pictures, sharing with friends and family, torch to light dark roads, maps, checking flight/train times, find hotels and many other things. Use these smart alternatives to traditional items like books to eliminate weight and save space.

I get ideas about what's essential when packing my suitcase.

-Diane von Furstenberg

TRAVELLING WITH KIDS

25. BRING ALONG THE STROLLER

Kids might enjoy walking for a while but they soon tire out and a stroller is the just the right thing for them to rest in while you continue your tour. Strollers also double duty as a luggage carrier and shopping bag holder. Remember to pick a light weight, easy to handle brand of stroller. Better yet, find out in advance if you can rent a stroller at your destination.

26. BRING ONLY ENOUGH DIAPERS FOR YOUR TRIP

Diapers take up a lot of space and add to the weight of your luggage. Therefore it is advisable to carry just enough diapers to last through the trip and a few for afterwards, till you buy fresh stock at your destination. Unless of course you are travelling to a really remote area, in which case you have no choice but to carry the load. Otherwise diapers are something you will find pretty easily.

27. TAKE ONLY A COUPLE OF TOYS

Children are easily attracted by new things in their environment. While travelling they will find numerous 'new' objects to scrutinize and play with. Packing just one favorite toy is enough, or if there is no favorite toy leave out all of them in favor of stories or imaginary games.

28. CARRY KID FRIENDLY SNACKS

Create a small snack counter in your bag to store away quick bites for those sudden hunger pangs. Depending on the child's age this could include chocolates, raisins, dry fruits, granola bars or biscuits. Also keep a bottle of water handy for your little one.

These things do not add much weight and can be adjusted in a handbag or knapsack.

29. GAMES TO CARRY

Create some travel specific, imaginary games if you have slightly grown up children, like spot the attractions. Keep a coloring book and colors handy for in-flight or hotel time. Apps on your smart phone can keep the children engaged with cartoons and story books. Older children are often entertained by games available on phones or tablets. This cuts the weight of luggage down while keeping the kids entertained.

30. LET THE KIDS CARRY THEIR LOAD

A good thing is to start early sharing of responsibilities. Let your child pick a bag of his or her choice and pack it themselves. Keep tabs on what they are stuffing in their bags by asking if they will be using that item on the trip. It could start out being just an entertainment bag initially but with growing years they will learn to sort the useful from the superfluous. Children as little as four can maneuver a small trolley suitcase like a pro- their experience in pull along toys credit. If you are worried that you may be pulling it for them, you may want to start with a backpack.

31. DECIDE ON LOCATION FOR CHILDREN TO SLEEP

While on a trip you might not always get a crib at your destination, and carrying one will make life all the more difficult. Instead call ahead to see if there are any cribs or roll out beds for children. You may even put blankets on the floor. Weave them a story about camping and they will gladly sleep without any trouble.

32. GET BABY PRODUCTS DELIVERED AT YOUR DESTINATION

If you are absolutely paranoid about not getting your favourite variety of diaper or brand of baby food, check out online stores like amazon.com for services in your destination city. You can buy things online ahead of your travel and get them delivered to your hotel upon arrival.

33. FEEDING NEEDS OF YOUR INFANTS

If you are travelling with a breastfed infant, you save the trouble of carrying bottles and bottle sanitization kits. For special food, or medications, you may need to call ahead to make sure you have a refrigerator where you are staying.

34. FEEDING NEEDS OF YOUR TODDLER

With the progression from infancy to toddler, their dietary requirements too evolve. You will have to pack some snacks for travelling time. Fresh fruits and vegetables can be purchased at your destination. Most of the cities you travel to in whichever part of the world, will have baby food products and formulas, available at the local drug-store or the supermarket.

35. PICKING CLOTHES FOR YOUR BABY

Contrary to popular belief, babies can do without many changes of clothes. At the most pack 2 outfits per day. Pack mix and match type clothes for your little one as well. Pick things which are comfortable to wear and quick to dry.

36. SELECTING SHOES FOR YOUR BABY

Like outfits, kids can make do with two pairs of comfortable shoes. If you can get some water resistant shoes it will be best. To expedite drying wet shoes, you can stuff newspaper in them then wrap them with newspaper and leave them to dry overnight.

37. KEEP ONE CHANGE OF CLOTHES HANDY

Travelling with kids can be tricky. Keep a change of clothes for the kids and mum handy in your purse or tote bag. This takes a bit of space in your hand luggage but comes extremely handy in case there are any accidents or spills.

38. LEAVE BEHIND BABY ACCESSORIES

Baby accessories like their bed, bath tub, car seat, crib etc. should be left at home. Many hotels provide a crib on request, while car seats can be borrowed from friends or rented. Babies can be given a bath in the hotel sink or even in the adult bath tub with a little bit of water. If you bring a few bath toys, they can be used in the bath, pool, and out of water. They can also be sanitized easily in the sink.

39. CARRY A SMALL LOAD OF PLASTIC BAGS

With children around there are chances of a number of soiled clothes and diapers. These plastic bags help to sort the dirt from the clean inside your big bag.

These are very light weight and come in handy to other carry stuff as well at times.

PACK WITH A PURPOSE

40. PACKING FOR BUSINESS TRIPS

One neutral-colored suit should suffice. It can be paired with different shirts, ties and accessories for different occasions. One pair of black suit pants could be worn with a matching jacket for the office or with a snazzy top for dinner.

41. PACKING FOR A CRUISE

Most cruises have formal dinners, and that formal dress usually takes up a lot of space. However you might find a tuxedo to rent. For women, a short black dress with multiple accessory options will do the trick.

42. PACKING FOR A LONG TRIP OVER DIFFERENT CLIMATES

The secret packing mantra for travel over multiple climates is layering. Layering traps air around your body creating insulation against the cold. The same light t-shirt that is comfortable in a warmer climate can be the innermost layer in a colder climate.

REDUCE SOME MORE WEIGHT

43. LEAVE PRECIOUS THINGS AT HOME

Things that you would hate to lose or get damaged leave them at home. Precious jewelry, expensive gadgets or dresses, could be anything. You will not require these on your trip. Leave them at home and spare the load on your mind.

44. SEND SOUVENIRS BY MAIL

If you have spent all your money on purchasing souvenirs, carrying them back in the same bag that you brought along would be difficult. Either pack everything in another bag and check it in the airport or get everything shipped to your home. Use an international carrier for a secure transit, but this could be more expensive than the checking fees at the airport.

45. AVOID CARRYING BOOKS

Books equal to weight. There are many reading apps which you can download on your smart phone or tab.

Plus there are gadgets like Kindle and Nook that are thinner and lighter alternatives to your regular book.

CHECK, GET, SET, CHECK AGAIN

46. STRATEGIZE BEFORE PACKING

Create a travel list and prepare all that you think you need to carry along. Keep everything on your bed or floor before packing and then think through once again – do I really need that? Any item that meets this question can be avoided. Remove whatever you don't really need and pack the rest.

47. TEST YOUR LUGGAGE

Once you have fully packed for the trip take a test trip with your luggage. Take your bags and go to town for window shopping for an hour. If you enjoy your hour long trip it is good to go, if not, go home and reduce the load some more. Repeat this test till you hit the right weight.

48. ADD A ROLL OF DUCT TAPE

You might wonder why, when this book has been talking about reducing stuff, we're suddenly asking you to pack something totally unusual. This is because when you have limited supplies, duct tape is immensely helpful for small repairs – a broken bag, leaking zip-lock bag, broken sunglasses, you name it and duct tape can fix it, temporarily.

49. LIST OF ESSENTIAL ITEMS

Even though the emphasis is on packing light, there are things which have to be carried for any trip. Here is our list of essentials:

•Passport/Visa or any other ID

•Any other paper work that might be required on a trip like permits, hotel reservation confirmations etc.

•Medicines – all your prescription medicines and emergency kit, especially if you are travelling with children

•Medical or vaccination records

•Money in foreign currency if travelling to a different country

•Tickets- Email or Message them to your phone

50. MAKE THE MOST OF YOUR TRIP

Wherever you are going, whatever you hope to do we encourage you to embrace it whole-heartedly. Take in the scenery, the culture and above all, enjoy your time away from home.

On a long journey even a straw weighs heavy.

-Spanish Proverb

PACKING AND PLANNING TIPS

A Week before Leaving

- Arrange for someone to take care of pets and water plants.

- Stop mail and newspaper.

- Notify Credit Card companies where you are going.

- Change your thermostat settings.

- Car inspected, oil is changed, and tires have the correct pressure.

- Passports and photo identification is up to date.

- Pay bills.

- Copy important items and download travel Apps.

- Start collecting small bills for tips.

Right Before Leaving

- Clean out refrigerator.

- Empty garbage cans.

- Lock windows.

- Make sure you have the proper identification with you.

- Bring cash for tips.

- Remember travel documents.

- Lock door behind you.

- Remember wallet.

- Unplug items in house and pack chargers.

>TOURIST

READ OTHER
GREATER THAN A TOURIST
BOOKS

Greater Than a Tourist San Miguel de Allende Guanajuato Mexico:
50 Travel Tips from a Local by Tom Peterson

Greater Than a Tourist – Lake George Area New York USA:
50 Travel Tips from a Local by Janine Hirschklau

Greater Than a Tourist – Monterey California United States:
50 Travel Tips from a Local by Katie Begley

Greater Than a Tourist – Chanai Crete Greece:
50 Travel Tips from a Local by Dimitra Papagrigoraki

Greater Than a Tourist – The Garden Route Western Cape Province
South Africa: 50 Travel Tips from a Local by Li-Anne McGregor van
Aardt

Greater Than a Tourist – Sevilla Andalusia Spain:
50 Travel Tips from a Local by Gabi Gazon

Greater Than a Tourist – Kota Bharu Kelantan Malaysia:
50 Travel Tips from a Local by Aditi Shukla

Children's Book: Charlie the Cavalier Travels the World by Lisa
Rusczyk

> TOURIST

Visit Greater Than a Tourist for Free Travel Tips
http://GreaterThanATourist.com

Sign up for the Greater Than a Tourist Newsletter for
discount days, new books, and travel information:
http://eepurl.com/cxspyf

Follow us on Facebook for tips, images, and ideas:
https://www.facebook.com/GreaterThanATourist

Follow us on Pinterest for travel tips and ideas:
http://pinterest.com/GreaterThanATourist

Follow us on Instagram for beautiful travel images:
http://Instagram.com/GreaterThanATourist

>TOURIST

> TOURIST

Please leave your honest review of this book on Amazon and Goodreads. Please send your feedback to GreaterThanaTourist@gmail.com as we continue to improve the series. We appreciate your positive and constructive feedback. Thank you.

METRIC CONVERSIONS

TEMPERATURE

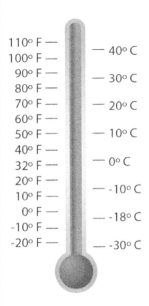

110° F —	— 40° C
100° F —	
90° F —	— 30° C
80° F —	
70° F —	— 20° C
60° F —	
50° F —	— 10° C
40° F —	
32° F —	— 0° C
20° F —	
10° F —	— -10° C
0° F —	— -18° C
-10° F —	
-20° F —	— -30° C

To convert F to C:

Subtract 32, and then multiply by 5/9 or .5555.

To Convert C to F:

Multiply by 1.8 and then add 32.

32F = 0C

LIQUID VOLUME

To Convert:.................Multiply by

U.S. Gallons to Liters................ 3.8
U.S. Liters to Gallons 26
Imperial Gallons to U.S. Gallons 1.2
Imperial Gallons to Liters....... 4.55
Liters to Imperial Gallons 22

1 Liter = .26 U.S. Gallon
1 U.S. Gallon = 3.8 Liters

DISTANCE

To convert ....Multiply by

Inches to Centimeters 2.54
Centimeters to Inches 39
Feet to Meters...................... .3
Meters to Feet 3.28
Yards to Meters 91
Meters to Yards 1.09
Miles to Kilometers 1.61
Kilometers to Miles............ .62

1 Mile = 1.6 km
1 km = .62 Miles

WEIGHT

1 Ounce = .28 Grams
1 Pound = .4555 Kilograms
1 Gram = .04 Ounce
1 Kilogram = 2.2 Pounds

TRAVEL QUESTIONS

- Do you bring presents home to family or friends after a vacation?

- Do you get motion sick?

- Do you have a favorite billboard?

- Do you know what to do if there is a flat tire?

- Do you like a sun roof open?

- Do you like to eat in the car?

- Do you like to wear sun glasses in the car?

- Do you like toppings on your ice cream?

- Do you use public bathrooms?

- Did you bring your cell phone and does it have power?

- Do you have a form of identification with you?

- Have you ever been pulled over by a cop?

- Have you ever given money to a stranger on a road trip?

- Have you ever taken a road trip with animals?

- Have you ever went on a vacation alone?

- Have you ever run out of gas?

- If you could move to any place in the world, where would it be?

- If you could travel anywhere in the world, where would you travel?

- If you could travel in any vehicle, which one would it be?

- If you had three things to wish for from a magic genie, what would they be?

- If you have a driver's license, how many times did it take you to pass the test?

- What are you the most afraid of on vacation?

- What do you want to get away from the most when you are on vacation?

- What foods smells bad to you?

- What item do you bring on ever trip with you away from home?

- What makes you sleepy?

- What song would you love to hear on the radio when you're cruising on the highway?

- What travel job would you want the least?

- What will you miss most while you are away from home?

- What is something you always wanted to try?

- What is the best road side attraction that you ever saw?

- What is the farthest distance you ever biked?

- What is the farthest distance you ever walked?

- What is the weirdest thing you needed to buy while on vacation?

- What is your favorite candy?

- What is your favorite color car?

- What is your favorite family vacation?

- What is your favorite food?

- What is your favorite gas station drink or food?

- What is your favorite license plate design?

- What is your favorite restaurant?

- What is your favorite smell?

- What is your favorite song?

- What is your favorite sound that nature makes?

- What is your favorite thing to bring home from a vacation?

- What is your favorite vacation with friends?

- What is your favorite way to relax?

- Where is the farthest place you ever traveled in a car?

- Where is the farthest place you ever went North, South, East and West?

- Where is your favorite place in the world?

- Who is your favorite singer?

- Who taught you how to drive?

- Who will you miss the most while you are away?

- Who if the first person you will contact when you get to your destination?

- Who brought you on your first vacation?

- Who likes to travel the most in your life?

- Would you rather be hot or cold?

- Would you rather drive above, below, or at the speed limited?

- Would you rather drive on a highway or a back road?

- Would you rather go on a train or a boat?

- Would you rather go to the beach or the woods?

TRAVEL BUCKET LIST

1.

2.

3.

4.

5.

6.

7.

8.

9.

10.

NOTES

Made in United States
North Haven, CT
26 June 2022

20629366R00071